THE UNITED STATES ENTERS THE 20th CENTURY

1890 to 1930

by DeAnn Herringshaw

HISTORY DIGS

CHERRY LAKE PUBLISHING • ANN ARBOR, MICHIGAN

Published in the United States of America
by Cherry Lake Publishing
Ann Arbor, Michigan
www.cherrylakepublishing.com

Printed in the United States of America
Corporate Graphics Inc
September 2011
CLFA09

Content Consultants: Michelle Kuhl, associate professor of history, University of Wisconsin Oshkosh; Gail Saunders-Smith, associate professor of literacy, Beeghly College of Education, Youngstown State University

Editorial direction:
Rebecca Rowell

Design and production:
Marie Tupy

Photo credits: Harris & Ewing, Washington, DC/Library of Congress, cover, 1; Underwood & Underwood/Library of Congress, 5, 24, 30; Lewis Wickes Hine/Library of Congress, 7, 13, 21; Library of Congress, 9, 10, 18; Lewis W. Hine/AP Images, 14; Fotosearch/Getty Images, 17; Royal L. Wolcott/Library of Congress, 22; Rare Book and Special Collections Division/Library of Congress, 27

Copyright ©2012 by Cherry Lake Publishing
All rights reserved. No part of this book may be reproduced or utilized in any form or by any means without written permission from the publisher.

Library of Congress Cataloging-in-Publication Data
Herringshaw, DeAnn, 1962-
 The United States enters the 20th century / by DeAnn Herringshaw.
  p. cm. – (Language arts explorer–History digs)
 ISBN 978-1-61080-200-0 – ISBN 978-1-61080-288-8 (pbk.)
 1. United States–History–1865-1921–Juvenile literature. 2. United States–History–1919-1933--Juvenile literature. 3. Progressivism (United States politics)–Juvenile literature. 4. United States–Politics and government–1865-1933–Juvenile literature. I. Title.
 E661.H47 2011
 973.91–dc22
                    2011015125

Cherry Lake Publishing would like to acknowledge the work of The Partnership for 21st Century Skills. Please visit www.21stCenturySkills.org for more information.

TABLE OF CONTENTS

Your Mission 4
What You Know 4
The Progressive Era Project 6
Women's Suffrage 9
Child Labor 12
African American Rights 16
Pure Food and Drug Act 20
Saving the Environment 23
Mission Accomplished! 26
Consider This 26
Glossary 28
Learn More 29
Further Missions 30
Index 31

You are being given a mission. The facts in **What You Know** will help you accomplish it. Remember the clues from **What You Know** while you are reading the story. The clues and the story will help you answer the questions at the end of the book. Have fun on this adventure!

YOUR MISSION

Your mission is to learn to think like a historian. What tools do historians use to research the past? What kinds of questions do they ask, and where do they look for answers? On this assignment, your goal is to investigate U.S. history between 1890 and 1930. This was a time of great change and many **reforms** in the country. Many of these changes were led by a group of people called the **Progressives**. Who were the Progressives? What problems did they face? What solutions did they find? As you read, keep What You Know in mind.

WHAT YOU KNOW

- ★ Progressives were people who believed in change. They were called reformers.
- ★ Theodore Roosevelt was a Progressive who wanted to stop mistreatment of the land and the people of America, especially by businesses.
- ★ Child labor, poor working conditions, unequal rights, unsafe food, and the destruction of the environment were all problems during this time.

Use this book to explore history in ways a historian might. Read the following journal to discover what one student learned about this time period while spending spring break with an aunt who is a historian.

President Theodore Roosevelt was a Progressive.

Entry 1: THE PROGRESSIVE ERA PROJECT

Today is the first day of spring break. I am staying for a week with my aunt, who is a historian at a museum. She is creating **exhibits** about the Progressive era in U.S. history, and I get to help her! We will be looking through the **archives** in the basement for all kinds of **artifacts**, such as old photographs, posters, and newspaper articles.

Theodore Roosevelt

In my aunt's office, I see a big picture of Theodore Roosevelt, who was president of the United States from 1901 to 1909. Under his picture are these words:

> We who stand for the Progressive movement . . . are pledged to eternal war against **tyranny** and wrong. . . . We stand for justice and for fair play. . . . We fight to make this country a better place to live in for those who have been harshly treated. . . . Surely there was never a more noble cause.

"Teddy Roosevelt was a Progressive, right?" I ask my aunt.

Long Hours, Little Pay

"Yes," she says. "When the United States was a young country, there were few laws to protect the land or the powerless—such as women, children, minorities, and the poor. Many businesspeople took advantage of their power and freedom to make a lot of money."

"How did they do that?" I ask.

This photograph shows how one woman struggled to survive in her poverty-stricken home by finishing pants. There is a stack of pants for her to work on as she and her children suffer from hunger.

"Well," she says, "bosses made their employees work very long hours. Many worked 12 hours a day. Some people worked up to 18 hours a day—even children—and very few bosses paid their employees a living wage."

"What's a living wage?" I ask.

"A living wage means that a worker earns enough money to buy basic things such as food, clothing, shelter, health care, education, and even a little entertainment," she explains. "The United States didn't have any wage laws, so bosses could pay as little as they wanted."

PROGRESSIVES TODAY

Many of the issues Progressives faced at the beginning of the twentieth century are still issues today. Modern Progressives believe the government should enact laws that protect the poor, the powerless, and the environment. Some progressive projects today include ensuring all Americans have good health care and protecting the environment.

"I bet there were a lot of poor people," I say.

"That's right." my aunt says. "Millions of people worked very hard and still couldn't afford to care for their families."

"And the bosses probably got really rich!" I exclaim.

"Right again," says my aunt. "As the rich grew richer, the poor grew poorer. Look at these photos." She shows me pictures of people living in miserable poverty.

"Why didn't rich people help them?" I ask.

"Many rich folks believed the poor deserved to be miserable. They thought poor people were lazy, stupid, or weak."

"That's not fair!" I say.

My aunt smiles. "The Progressives also thought it wasn't fair. They wanted laws to protect the poor. They wanted America to be a true democracy for everyone, not only for a few. Roosevelt helped make that happen."

"How did the Progressives change this?" I ask my aunt.

"You'll see," she says. "Let's get started." ★

Entry 2: WOMEN'S SUFFRAGE

We're in the archives looking for artifacts. I find an old printed paper with a drawing of a woman riding a white horse. It says "Woman Suffrage" on it. I show it to my aunt.

"Wow!" she says. "This is the program for the women's suffrage parade in Washington, DC, on March 3, 1913."

"What's suffrage?" I ask.

This artifact is the official program of the women's suffrage parade held in Washington, DC, on March 3, 1913.

Women Unequal

"The right to vote," my aunt tells me. "One hundred years ago, women were not allowed to vote in the states, though a few territories allowed women to vote. For thousands of years, men believed women were **inferior**. Women had little or no control over their property, and they had few legal rights."

"That's not fair!" I say.

"No, it wasn't," my aunt agrees. "Women had no power in government. And many were discouraged from going to college or getting an education."

"Why?" I ask.

"If women became educated, they'd fight for their rights," she says. "And that's exactly what happened," she explains. "Some women became educated, wrote about women's rights, and demanded the right to vote. These women were called suffragists."

Fighting for the Right to Vote

Next, I find an old newspaper called *Woman's Journal and Suffrage News*. On the front page are photographs of women in a parade. I read the headline aloud: "Parade Struggles to Victory Despite Disgraceful Scenes."

"This is about the parade on March 3, 1913." I show it to my aunt. "What were the 'disgraceful scenes'?"

"Read and find out," she says.

The article says thousands of women were marching peacefully when they were attacked. Anti-suffragists spat at, slapped, and threw cigar butts at marchers. The police didn't protect the marchers, which made the public very angry. It actually caused more people to join the cause for women's rights.

My aunt points to the newspaper. "That woman riding the white horse was Inez Milholland. Her parents were wealthy Progressives. She was a lawyer. She and her father fought for equal rights for African Americans, too."

"Did women win the right to vote after the parade?" I ask.

"Not right away," my aunt says. "It took years of marches, speeches, and protests before women won the right to vote. A lot of people didn't want it to happen."

"Well, when did women finally get to vote?" I ask impatiently.

"It happened slowly, state by state. And in August 1920, Congress **ratified** the Nineteenth Amendment to the Constitution. In November 1920, women across the United States voted for the first time in a national election. However, many African American women were kept from voting because of their race. This changed later in the twentieth century." ★

THE EQUAL RIGHTS AMENDMENT

In 1923, suffragist Alice Paul wrote the Equal Rights Amendment (ERA), which would give women and men equal rights under the law. It states, "Men and women shall have equal rights throughout the United States and every place subject to its jurisdiction." As of early 2011, the ERA had not yet been ratified.

Entry 3: CHILD LABOR

It's the second day of our project. Today, I find several photographs of children working in terrible places doing very hard jobs.

"What are these kids doing?" I ask.

Helping Their Families

"These are child laborers," my aunt says. "Many little children worked to help support their families in those days. Why do think that was?"

"Because bosses didn't pay their parents enough?" I ask.

"Exactly!" she says. "Some parents worked very hard, but they couldn't earn enough money to support their families. And some parents were sick, unable to work, gone, or dead. So, the children had to go to work instead of school. In farming societies, it was normal for children to work on the farm with their parents. That way, they learned to farm and helped out the family. When families moved to cities, they thought it was normal for children to work. But factory work was much harder and less safe than farm work. And children were not learning many skills for a good adult job."

Benefits of Hiring Children

"Why would someone want to hire kids?" I ask.

"Children have nimble little hands for working with small tools," my aunt explains. "They learned quickly and would work for much lower wages than adults."

"Some of the children in these photos were really little," I say. "They should have been in school, not working."

Boys ranging in age from seven to 12 worked at a canning company in Maine, usually earning 75 cents for working from 7:00 a.m. until midnight.

"Yes. Children as young as five worked all day and even at night," she explains. "They developed diseases from breathing polluted air in factories and coal mines. They couldn't go to school, so many were illiterate—they couldn't read or write. Worst of all, many were injured or killed while working in dangerous conditions."

"That's horrible!" I cry.

"Yes, it was," she agrees. "Progressives believed all children deserved an education so they could grow up to be healthy, productive adults. They believed child labor was the greatest evil in our nation."

Regulating Child Labor

"How did they fight it?" I ask.

"In 1904, some Progressive reformers created the National Child Labor Committee," she tells me. "They sent investigators to gather evidence. Lewis Hine was a photographer who took thousands of photographs of children all over the United States. Bosses tried to

Six-year-old Laura Petty was photographed by Lewis Hine on July 7, 1909. The little girl worked as a berry picker in Rock Creek, Maryland, and was taking a break.

CHILD LABOR TODAY

Child labor is now illegal in many nations, but it is still happening in parts of Asia, Africa, and South America. In 2008, at least 150 million children worked long hours in unsafe conditions. Many toys and clothing items in U.S. stores are made by children who work instead of attending school. Today, many companies and consumers are choosing products that follow practices that avoid such labor, but the situation still exists.

stop Hine from taking pictures. They didn't want the public to find out how they were using children."

"Did he take pictures anyway?" I ask.

"Yes, secretly. When he published these pictures, the public was outraged and demanded that politicians stop child labor."

"Did it work?" I ask.

"Not right away," my aunt says. "Powerful businessmen who hired child workers influenced the politicians. They claimed the Progressives would ruin the country if they forced the government to regulate, or put controls on, business."

"Why didn't the president just **abolish** child labor?" I ask.

"That's not how laws are made in the United States," my aunt says. "Congress did pass a law against child labor, but the Supreme Court decided the Constitution did not allow for the law. The justices ruled the federal government should not interfere with labor."

"The Progressives didn't give up, did they?" I ask.

"No," my aunt says. "It took many years, but child labor was finally banned in 1938." ★

Entry 4: AFRICAN AMERICAN RIGHTS

Today, I find a booklet titled *Southern Horrors: Lynch Law in All its Phases* by Ida B. Wells-Barnett. The pamphlet talks about white people lynching African Americans. I show it to my aunt.

"What is lynching?" I ask her.

My aunt looks serious and sad. "Lynching is public murder by a group, usually by hanging or burning at the stake."

I'm shocked and horrified. "This happened in the United States?"

"Yes," she answers. "Many white people wanted to keep African Americans from gaining power. They used the lynch law to keep black people afraid."

Lynch Law

"What's the lynch law?" I ask.

"Lynch law stems from the idea that some people aren't full citizens. So, if they go against community standards, some people believe they aren't protected by the law. They don't stand before a jury at a trial. White Southerners did not believe African Americans deserved to be citizens and punished them with lynch law—just a mob who executed them without a judge, jury, or trial."

"Did these white people lynch only criminals?" I ask.

"No," my aunt says. "Many innocent people were lynched. Even if African Americans committed a crime, they had a legal right to a fair trial. But racists didn't want African Americans to have rights—so they lynched them."

"They killed people for no reason?" I ask.

THE NEW YORK TIMES, THURSDAY, NOVEMBER 23, 1922

THE SHAME OF AMERICA

Do you know that the United States is the Only Land on Earth where human beings are BURNED AT THE STAKE?

In Four Years, 1918-1921, Twenty-Eight People Were Publicly BURNED BY AMERICAN MOBS

3436 People Lynched 1889 to 1922

For What Crimes Have Mobs Nullified Government and Inflicted the Death Penalty?

The Alleged Crimes	The Victims
Murder	1288
Rape	571
Crimes against the Person	615
Crimes against Property	333
Miscellaneous Crimes	453
Absence of Crime	176
	3436

Why Some Mob Victims Died:
Not turning out of road for white boy in auto
Being a relative of a person who was lynched
Jumping a labor contract
Being a member of the Non-Partisan League
"Talking back" to a white man
"Insulting" white man.

Is Rape the "Cause" of Lynching?

Of 3,436 people murdered by mobs in our country, only 571, or less than 17 per cent., were even accused of the crime of rape.

83 WOMEN HAVE BEEN LYNCHED IN THE UNITED STATES

Do lynchers maintain that they were lynched for "the usual crime"?

AND THE LYNCHERS GO UNPUNISHED

THE REMEDY

The Dyer Anti-Lynching Bill Is Now Before the United States Senate

The Dyer Anti-Lynching Bill was passed on January 26, 1922, by a vote of 230 to 119 in the House of Representatives.

The Dyer Anti-Lynching Bill Provides:
That culpable State officers and mobbists shall be tried in Federal Courts on failure of State courts to act, and that a county in which a lynching occurs shall be fined $10,000, recoverable in a Federal Court.

The Principal Question Raised Against the Bill is upon the Ground of Constitutionality.

The Constitutionality of the Dyer Bill Has Been Affirmed by
The Judiciary Committee of the House of Representatives
The Judiciary Committee of the Senate
The United States Attorney General, legal advisor of Congress
Judge Guy D. Goff, of the Department of Justice

The Senate has been petitioned to pass the Dyer Bill by
29 Lawyers and Jurists, including two former Attorneys General of the United States
19 State Supreme Court Justices
24 State Governors
3 Archbishops, 85 bishops and prominent churchmen
39 Mayors of large cities, north and south.

The American Bar Association at its meeting in San Francisco, August 9, 1922, adopted a resolution asking for further legislation by Congress to punish and prevent lynching and mob violence.

Fifteen State Conventions of 1922, 3 of them Democratic have inserted in their party platforms a demand for national action to stamp out lynchings.

The Dyer Anti-Lynching Bill is not intended to protect the guilty, but to assure to every person accused of crime trial by due process of law.

THE DYER ANTI-LYNCHING BILL IS NOW BEFORE THE SENATE
TELEGRAPH YOUR SENATORS TODAY YOU WANT IT ENACTED

If you want to help the organization which has brought to light the facts about lynching, the organization which is fighting for 100 per cent Americanism, not for some of the people some of the time, but for all of the people, white or black, all of the time

Send your check to J. E. SPINGARN, Treasurer of the

NATIONAL ASSOCIATION FOR THE ADVANCEMENT OF COLORED PEOPLE
70 FIFTH AVENUE, NEW YORK CITY

THIS ADVERTISEMENT IS PAID FOR IN PART BY THE ANTI-LYNCHING CRUSADERS.

This advertisement for the Dyer Anti-Lynching Bill, published in the New York Times on November 23, 1922, gives a sense of what life was like during this period.

Ida B. Wells-Barnett fought for equal rights for African Americans.

"Oh, they gave many excuses for lynching," she explains. "If a black man looked at a white woman, the woman could accuse him of trying to hurt her. Some African Americans were lynched for trying to vote, for arguing with a white person, for protesting low wages, or for speaking out against racism."

Fighting Lynching and Forming the NAACP

"Did Progressives fight against lynching?" I ask.

My aunt shakes her head sadly. "African Americans were an important part of the Progressive movement. Still, many white Progressives were more concerned about other issues," she says. "But some white Progressives, such as Inez Milholland and her father, helped Wells-Barnett fight lynching."

"How did they fight it?" I ask.

"In 1909, the Milhollands and other white Progressive reformers joined Wells-Barnett and other African American leaders to establish the National Association for the Advancement of Colored People, or NAACP. The NAACP was created to fight all forms of racism and win equal rights for African Americans and all people of color."

"When did they abolish lynching?" I ask.

My aunt sighs. "The NAACP fought for more than 30 years to get anti-lynching laws passed. Look at this," she says.

She shows me an old newspaper and I read part of it aloud: "The Shame of America . . . 3436 People Lynched 1889 to 1922 . . ."

"The NAACP took out large advertisements like this in major magazines and newspapers asking people to tell their senators to vote for this anti-lynching bill," my aunt explains. "But many Southern senators refused to pass it. In fact, the Senate never passed any anti-lynching laws."

"Well, how did lynching end?" I ask.

"Lynching gradually stopped as African Americans began getting fair trials," she says. "The NAACP played a role by raising money to defend African Americans who couldn't afford good lawyers. The organization spoke out against all forms of racism in society, which helped educate white people about the evils of racism. The NAACP became a powerful force in the battle for civil rights—and it still fights racism today." ★

U.S. SENATE APOLOGIZES

In June 2005, the U.S. Senate apologized for never passing an anti-lynching law. The apology didn't help the thousands of African Americans who were lynched or the families who suffered. Perhaps the Senate's apology can help Americans remember how destructive racism is, so that things such as lynching will never happen again.

Entry 5: PURE FOOD AND DRUG ACT

Today, I find strange-looking advertisements for medicines such as "Pink Pills for Pale People" or "Snake Oil Cure!"

"What are these?" I ask my aunt.

Patent Medicines

"Advertisements for patent medicines," she says. "People used to make and sell all kinds of folk remedies, including pills, syrups, and oils. These so-called medicines were claimed to cure almost anything."

"Did they work?" I ask.

"No. Those medicines were just mixes of minerals, vegetables, or herbs, blended with alcohol or dangerous **narcotics**. Some cures for children's toothaches or stomach pains contained cocaine, heroin, or opium—dangerous drugs that are illegal today," my aunt tells me.

"Why would parents give these things to their children?" I ask.

"The medicine recipes were secret," my aunt says. "People didn't understand how dangerous they were. Some got addicted to the medicines. Some even died."

Regulating Foods and Drugs

Next, I find a newspaper article about Roosevelt signing the Pure Food and Drug **Act** of 1906. "What was this about?" I ask.

"Before Roosevelt signed this act, there were no laws to ensure that food and drugs were clean and safe. Slaughterhouses, the places where animals are butchered for meat, were filthy and dangerous. Consumers didn't know they were buying and eating contaminated, diseased, and rotten meat," my aunt tells me.

These women shelled nuts to earn money. The woman in white is cracking shells with her teeth, not eating nuts.

"That's disgusting!" I say.

"It wasn't only bad meat," my aunt says. "Food manufacturers put spoiled vegetables, fruits, milk, and grains in canned foods. Many people got sick and died from eating bad food."

"Why did companies sell rotten food?" I ask.

"Food producers would lose money if they threw away spoiled food. There was no law to stop them, so they processed and sold it."

Next, I find a photograph of a poor family shelling nuts. "What's going on here?" I ask

My aunt says, "Some people earned a little money by shelling nuts at home, but there was a risk there as well because the surroundings weren't always clean. Some cracked nuts with their teeth and picked the nuts from the shells with dirty fingers."

"That's terrible!" I say. "But did businessmen fight the Pure Food and Drug Act?"

"They sure did," my aunt says. "Roosevelt wanted to pass a strict law, but powerful businessmen pressured Congress to leave them alone. These **capitalists** knew they might not make as much money if the law was passed."

"What did Roosevelt do about it?" I ask.

"He let journalists publish a report from the Agriculture Department that described what the producers of food and medicine were doing. When the public found out, they pressured Congress to pass the Pure Food and Drug Act. Then, Roosevelt signed it into law."

"What did the new law say?" I ask.

"It said that anyone who sold meat from sick animals, put spoiled ingredients in any food, or used false advertising could be fined and jailed," says my aunt. "Drugs could only be sold by companies that followed standards of purity and safety, so patent medicines fell out of practice." ★

FOOD SAFETY

The Food and Drug Administration (FDA) is responsible for making sure U.S. food and medicine supplies are pure and safe. If a product is not safe, the FDA issues a recall and has products removed from stores. Recent food recalls include contaminated meat, eggs, milk, spinach, tomatoes, and even pet food.

Entry 6: SAVING THE ENVIRONMENT

It's the last day of spring break. I find a photograph of some men standing in front of a huge tree. "What kind of tree is this?" I ask my aunt. "It's gigantic!"

"That's a Sequoia—a giant redwood tree that grows in California," she says. "This was taken when Roosevelt went camping in the California mountains."

"The president went camping?" I ask.

Conserving Nature

"Yes," my aunt says. "He was a great conservationist, someone who loves nature and works to save it. Some people were getting rich taking whatever they wanted from the land—trees, animals, water, and minerals. The fashion industry drove several species of birds to the brink of extinction."

"That's weird! How did fashion destroy bird populations?" I ask.

"In those days, women wore hats piled high with bird feathers and even the bodies of whole birds," my aunt says. "Every year, hunters killed millions of birds to sell to the fashion industry. Feather traders got the highest prices for long, silky feathers from large water birds. Whooping cranes, snowy egrets, and herons were nearly wiped out."

"How were they saved?" I ask.

"In 1902, Roosevelt established the first bird preserve—a place where hunting was not allowed. Anyone caught killing birds there could be jailed or fined. Roosevelt established 51 preserves where birds could safely raise their young."

This photograph captured Roosevelt visiting California. He and his party were dwarfed by a massive redwood.

Theodore Roosevelt and John Muir

I find a photograph of Roosevelt standing on a mountain next to a man with a long beard. "Who is this?" I ask my aunt.

"That's John Muir," she says, "a famous naturalist and writer. Roosevelt admired Muir's work and invited him to go camping to discuss environmental issues."

"What kind of issues?" I ask.

"Issues such as how to preserve large areas of natural wilderness for future generations," my aunt answers. "Both men believed it was important for humans to explore and enjoy nature. They also knew something needed to be done or there would be no more wild, beautiful places left."

"How did they save nature?" I ask.

"Muir convinced Roosevelt to add more land to Yosemite National Park to protect it from loggers who were destroying many forests. Then, Roosevelt created five national parks and 150 national forests, ultimately setting aside more than 200 million acres of land for conservation." ★

CLEAR-CUTTING

Clear-cutting is when loggers cut down and remove all trees from a section of a forest. It is faster and easier to clear-cut land than it is to select and cut only certain trees in a forest. However, environmentalists argue the practice is bad for the environment because it destroys existing habitats and increases soil erosion. Many environmentalists want Congress to pass laws against clear-cutting in U.S. parks and forests.

MISSION ACCOMPLISHED!

Congratulations! You have learned about some of the many changes that took place at the beginning of the twentieth century. You have discovered how Progressives fought for women's suffrage and against child labor. Some Progressives helped white Americans realize they didn't treat people fairly. You have also learned how the government made laws to keep food and medicine pure. Also, you have explored how the government saved lands for future generations. Good job!

CONSIDER THIS

★ How have children's lives changed in the past 100 years?

★ How would your life be different if you had been born before the Progressive era?

★ What else could Progessives have done to stop lynching?

★ If you were a Progressive at the beginning of the twentieth century, what else might have you worked toward improving?

★ How have parks and forests made life better for all Americans?

PLATFORM
of the
National Progressive Party
of the
State of New York

Adopted by the State Convention, Syracuse, N. Y., Sept. 5th, 1912

We, the National Progressive Party, in State convention assembled, ratify and reaffirm our national platform, and pledge our support to its candidates, Theodore Roosevelt, for President, and Hiram W. Johnson, for Vice-President. The hopes of a generation are realized in the birth of the new party.

Unhampered by any corrupt political past, or by that "invisible government," which has so long coerced legislation to serve special and private interests, we present our first State ticket. In no other State of the Union can citizens place as little trust and hope in the old parties as in New York. Between the "Old Guard," which fought Governor Hughes with Democratic aid, and the Tammany machine dominating Governor Dix with Republican aid, there is no choice. Each promises reforms at conventions and forgets them at Albany.

We pledge ourselves to the elimination of special privilege in every form. We covenant unceasing war against the use of political or governmental power for the private gain of bosses or their friends, who would build up great individual fortunes through monopoly, high prices, and inordinate profits.

We propose to use the powers of the government to protect property rights no less than heretofore, but seek also to serve human welfare more. We covenant with the people as follows:

The Rule of the People

(1.) A Real Direct Primary Law

We denounce the so-called Direct Primary Act of 1911 as a deliberate attempt to discredit the principle of direct nominations and retain boss control.

We pledge the enactment of a real Direct Primary Law applicable to every elective office, and a presidential preference primary law.

(2.) The Election Law

We denounce the Levy Election Law as a bi-partisan conspiracy; we pledge its repeal and the enactment of a fair and understandable statute.

(3) Direct Election of United States Senators

We favor the election of United States Senators by direct vote of the people.

(4.) An Office Group Ballot For All Elections

We favor the type of Massachusetts ballot.

This is the platform adopted by the New York State chapter of the National Progressive Party on September 5, 1912.

abolish (uh-BAH-lish) to get rid of something completely

act (akt) a bill that Congress has approved and that will become a law if the president signs it

archive (AHR-kive) a place where historical documents are stored safely

artifact (ARH-tuh-fakt) an object made by people in the past

capitalist (KAP-i-tuh-list) someone who believes in making money for personal gain

exhibit (ig-ZIB-it) a collection of objects placed in a public area for people to see

inferior (in-FEER-ee-ur) of less importance or value

narcotic (nahr-KAH-tik) an addictive drug that makes people very sleepy and takes away pain

Progressive (pruh-GRES-iv) a group that supports change, especially in terms of education, society, and politics; a member of this group

ratify (RAT-uh-fye) to make a bill into law by signing it or voting for it

reform (ri-FORM) a change made to improve or correct something

tyranny (TIR-uh-nee) cruel and unfair treatment of people by those in power

LEARN MORE

BOOKS

Bartoletti, Susan Campbell. *Kids on Strike!* Boston, MA: Sandpiper, 2003.

Freedman, Russell. *Kids at Work: Lewis Hine and the Crusade Against Child Labor.* New York, NY: Clarion, 1994.

Kamma, Anne. *If You Lived When Women Won Their Rights.* New York, NY: Scholastic, 2008.

Myers, Walter Dean. *Ida B. Wells: Let the Truth Be Told.* New York, NY: Amistad, 2008.

Rohmer, Harriet. *Heroes of the Environment: True Stories of People Who are Helping to Protect Our Planet.* San Francisco, CA: Chronicle Books, 2009.

WEB SITES

America's Story from America's Library
http://www.americaslibrary.gov/

Read stories of great Americans, play fun games, and explore every era of U.S. history at this Library of Congress site.

National Museum of American History: Kenneth E. Behring Center
http://americanhistory.si.edu/kids/

Explore this Smithsonian site to learn about history, discover great books, and find learning activities and crafts to do at home.

FURTHER MISSIONS

MISSION 1

Imagine that you have traveled back in time to the Progressive era, sometime between 1890 and 1930. Maybe you have to find a job to support yourself, such as by selling newspapers on the streets or working in a factory. Write about what life is like for you and the other children you meet.

MISSION 2

Create a comic book or series of drawings about what you would do if you were a reformer. You may want to imagine yourself as a Progressive era reformer or someone concerned about reforming the world today. Think about the things that matter to you the most. What would you like to change? Create a world where you solve those problems.

INDEX

African American rights, 16, 18–19

birds, 23

canned foods, 21
child labor, 4, 12–15, 26
clear-cutting, 25
conserving nature, 23
Constitution, 11, 15

Equal Rights Amendment, 11

Food and Drug Administration (FDA), 22

Hine, Lewis, 14–15

lynch law, 16, 18

Milholland, Inez, 11, 18
Muir, John, 24–25

National Association for the Advancement of Colored People (NAACP), 18–19
National Child Labor Committee, 14
Nineteenth Amendment, 11

patent medicines, 20, 22
Paul, Alice, 11
pay, 7, 12
poverty, 8
Progressives, 4, 8, 11, 13, 15, 18, 26
Pure Food and Drug Act of 1906, 20–22

Roosevelt, Theodore, 4, 6, 8, 20, 22, 23, 24–25

slaughterhouses, 20

Wells-Barnett, Ida B., 16, 18
Woman's Journal and Suffrage News, 10–11
women's suffrage, 9–11, 26

ABOUT THE AUTHOR

DeAnn Herringshaw enjoys researching and writing books for children and adults. She is a mother of four grown children. DeAnn enjoys gardening, hiking, and horses. She lives in St. Paul, Minnesota, with her youngest son and a cat.

ABOUT THE CONSULTANTS

Michelle Kuhl grew up in North Carolina, went to upstate New York for her history PhD, taught in Texas for two years, and currently works at the University of Wisconsin Oshkosh. She has two daughters: one who thinks she is a fairy princess, and one who thinks she is a descendent of a Greek god. Both of them like going to the library with their mortal mom.

Gail Saunders-Smith is a former classroom teacher and Reading Recovery teacher leader. Currently, she teaches literacy courses at Youngstown State University in Ohio. Gail is the author of many books for children and three professional books for teachers.